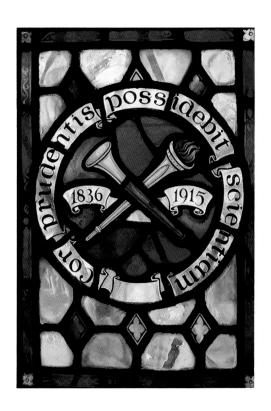

*My impression of Emory is that you are doing the required work of a university amazingly well, and with astounding modesty, as compared with some other institutions. I believe it more nearly approaches Dr. Abraham Flexner's "ideal university" than any other institution in America.*

Edwin R. Embree, February 1931
Southern Conference on Education

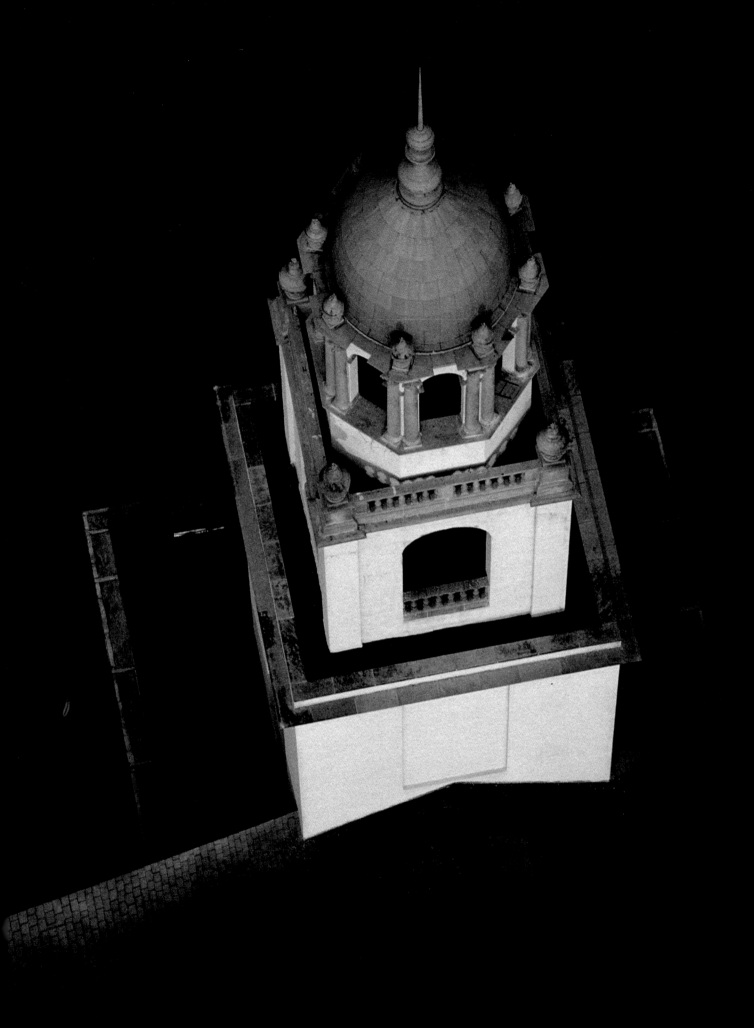

# EMORY

## UNIVERSITY

PHOTOGRAPHED BY TOMMY L. THOMPSON

HARMONY HOUSE

PUBLISHERS LOUISVILLE

Executive Editors: William Butler and William Strode
Director of Photography: William Strode
Library of Congress Catalog Number 86-082745
Hardcover International Standard Book Number 0-916509-23-0
Printed in U.S.A. by Pinaire Lithographing Corp., Louisville, Kentucky
First Edition November, 1987
Published by Harmony House Publishers, P.O. Box 90, Prospect, Kentucky 40059
(502) 228-2010 / 228-4446
Copyright © 1987 by Harmony House Publishers
Photographs copyright © 1987 by Tommy Thompson, '70C

*The William R. Cannon Chapel*

*The Pitts Theology Library*

# A SENSE OF LARGER PURPOSE

A Sesquicentennial Address  by Dr. James T. Laney

President, Emory University

The observance of a major anniversary in an institution's life is usually taken as a time to celebrate how far it has come from its beginnings, with appropriate festivities and often the trumpetings of progress. There is an inevitable tendency to patronize the past, which after all was long ago; our present is so vivid with its problems and opportunities, while the past, looked back upon from our lofty height, seems so modest. I think this tendency is particularly present with us at Emory. Our University indeed has had an impressive flowering in these last decades, especially since its transposition from Oxford to Atlanta, from college to university, from a place where everybody knew everybody to a place where there are scores of new faculty every year and students struggle to get acquainted with those in their own dorms.

We do have much to celebrate and much to be proud of and, if the truth were told, I'm as competitive as anyone and want Emory to be the best. But this Sesquicentennial year has provided an important opportunity for me and for others to ponder the past. In this quest I have re-read the two histories of the institution; the Thanksgiving sermon by Atticus Haygood; some of the correspondence between Bishop Warren Candler, an early president and later chancellor of the university, and his brother Asa, the founder of Coca-Cola. I've read reports of Dr. Cox and Dr. White. I've looked at the high points of the era of Henry Bowden and of the times of Dr. Martin and Dr. Atwood. And I have read Harvey Young's brief history. Out of this reading has arisen a fresh and vivid appreciation of those 150 years. What comes through so clearly is the really extraordinary personal investment of those early people, our predecessors — their vision, their courage, maybe most of all their doggedness, their persistence, their investment of themselves in something they would never see come to fruition. They were fired by a vision of training up generations of men, and then men and women, as one of the early people said, "fit for pulpit or plow, for court or camp, the Senate or the shop," educated in the best ways they knew at the time, and imbued with a sense of service and the conviction that good and useful lives required the fusion of knowledge and piety. This sense of larger purpose, of dedication, of commitment, was manifest from the beginning. And with all this was a vaulting sense of hope and perhaps a bit of vanity that encouraged them to give that little undeveloped plot of land outside of Covington the grand name of Oxford.

Emory was founded just as Alexis de Tocqueville published the first two volumes of his celebrated *Democracy in America*, in which he remarked on the unique spirit he found in this country that led people to devote their energies and fortunes in establishing private institutions and voluntary organizations to further the public good. De Tocqueville felt that this spirit, which did not exist in Europe, accounted for the extraordinary buoyancy and vitality of the young United States. Emory was to be a fine example of that hardy American phenomenon, whereby men and women came together to invest themselves beyond their own interests and affairs.

It certainly needed a hearty spirit, for the first years were a case study in hardship. Emory had been planted on the edge, literally, of a wilderness, before Atlanta was even founded in an area where higher education was at best dispensable and at worst despised. The new college was always short of funds. I read with eye-opening appreciation that the early presidents had to have at least one other job just to keep their families fed. Mark you, they were all talented men, with other opportunities available to them. Ignatius Few — I love these early names, Ignatius, Augustus, Atticus — Ignatius Few, the first president, was a graduate of Princeton, a planter, a colonel, a lawyer, and then a minister in that order. Few's successor, Augustus Longstreet, had gone to Yale, served as a judge of the Georgia Supreme Court and as publisher of an Augusta newspaper, was a noted essayist and author of *Georgia Scenes*, who in turn became also a Methodist minister.

Of course these early leaders were also creatures of the time. Emory, before the Civil War, was the intellectual center of Southern Methodism, after it withdrew from the church over slavery. Certainly up to and for some years after the Civil War it was touch-and-go for survival. The war left the college destitute and the South impoverished and devastated. But the region shortly began to recover, and one of the great forces in helping to recover was the leadership from Emory College.

Atticus Haygood, who was president during the decade 1875-1885, preached a remarkable Thanksgiving sermon in 1880 at the Old Church at Oxford, calling for the acceptance of the new state of affairs and for reconciliation with the North. Haygood acknowledged that abolition not only had been necessary but was also desirable and good, and he called upon the South to emerge from its ignorance and indifference and urged on it industry and economy. His speech was not very well received by his fellow Southerners, but the faculty thought it was splendid and asked to have it published. That was providential, because a copy of the speech fell into the hands of a Northern banker named George I. Seney. Seney was so impressed with Haygood's spirit of moderation and irenic tone, that he asked Emory's president to call upon him and ended up giving the College what was then a munificent sum totaling $130,000. And so just over a century ago, the college was put finally on a basic footing with total assets of $196,000.

This was the re-emergence of Emory as an effective leader in the region and in the state, progressive and courageous an educator of leaders. The college thrived under President Warren Candler, and for the first time we begin to see what

*Administration Building*

modest success can encourage in the way of vanity. There was a young Korean nobleman who was a student at Emory in the early 1890s, Yun Chiho, later Baron Yun. He was to become a distinguished leader and educator in Korea. In his diaries that he kept daily while he was a student at Oxford, Yun drew a fascinating picture of life out at old Emory. He wrote that one day there was a hotly contested debate on the topic "Resolved, that the non-white races are inferior," and he was relieved when there was an overwhelming victory against that position. Yun also wrote of having dinner with the Candlers one evening. After dinner, the president said, "While Emory is not yet as renowned as Harvard, academically it is comparable." Young Mr. Yun noted in his diary, "I left thinking he might have been somewhat swayed by his enthusiasm." That was not the last time a college president has been known to be swayed by his enthusiasm.

In the late 1890s, Emory professor Andrew Sledd published an article in the *Atlantic Monthly* attacking the notion of white supremacy. This caused a furor across the South. In order to avoid trouble for the college, Sledd voluntarily resigned from the faculty and moved on to become president of the University of Florida. A few years later, when Emory had moved to Atlanta, he took up his post again at Emory as professor of Greek and New Testament and was an early proponent of higher critical studies of the Bible. He established without question a firm precedent for untrammeled academic freedom that was later so staunchly upheld by President Atwood during the God-is-dead controversy.

There was another incident, modest in itself, which had far-reaching consequences for Emory as well, that had to do with upholding academic standards for students. It happened the day President James Dickey, our esteemed current board chairman's grandfather, decided that young Robert Woodruff had been at Emory long enough. Now one must remember, the Woodruffs were powerful even back then. Ernest Woodruff was one of the most important figures in this region. To send home the son was not exactly to befriend the father. I have often wondered if Robert Woodruff's profound respect for Emory didn't have something to do with that incident. For thirty years he refused the honorary degree that the Trustees had voted him. He only took it on his ninetieth birthday, and then with a touchingly humble acceptance. I'll have to tell you too that one day some years ago, when he was very alert and was telling me about his days at Oxford, I asked him somewhat impishly, "Mr. Woodruff, have you ever thought what you might have been able to accomplish had you finished Emory?" With a smile and an airy wave of his cigar, he said, "Yeah, I would have been four years behind."

So, we see Emory in successive stages from its birth in rural Georgia within the bosom of the church, to its growth as a progressive influence within the region, to its present dynamic partnership with the national and international city of Atlanta. We see its history as a progression of the generations that have gone forth from Emory, not only to Georgia, but across the country and throughout the world, as ministers, lawyers, physicians, business leaders, teachers, scholars, jurists, dentists, nurses, reaching the pinnacle of success in their various vocations:

bishops; heads of corporations; a Supreme Court justice of the United States; a vice president of the United States; members of Congress, including the two Georgia senators [now] in Washington, D.C. Four of this century's finest historians have come out of Emory College: Dumas Malone, David Potter, C. Vann Woodward, and Louis Harlan, all Pulitzer Prize winners. There have been legions of college and university presidents, including the first president of Georgia Tech, presidents of the universities of Chicago, Georgia, Mississippi, Florida, Miami, Texas A&M, and other institutions too numerous to mention.

And we can trace our history by the remarkable growth of this campus, fueled by the extraordinary philanthropy of the Candlers, then the Woodruffs, making possible a vast array of buildings, laboratories and libraries, hospitals and clinics, institutes and centers, with current assets of one and a half billion dollars and an endowment of just about half that much. And there are our centers for specialized research and study — the ILA, the Carter Center, Yerkes and many others — and also distinguished affiliates such as Scholars Press; the National Faculty for Humanities, Arts & Sciences; CDC; and The Southern Association, the latter organization accrediting from kindergarten to university, from Virginia to Texas. We are enriched by the resources of students from fifty states and over eighty countries, we have a distinguished and vigorous faculty, moving to take a lead in research and investigation, while continuing Emory's traditional strengths in teaching and clinical training.

And of course we are the only university in the country with a former United States president on its faculty. In this century there has been only one other, and that was Yale, which had William Howard Taft.

What is impressive in looking back on this growth is the spirit that made it possible. Each generation had its obstacles as it sought to shore up the College and enable it to flourish despite ignorance, inadequate financial support, and occasionally outright hostility. In the aftermath of civil war, there were the calls — courageous for that time — for reconciliation and justice for all peoples. There was the recurrent insistence on fairness-for-all against know-nothing-ism which keeps coming back in various forms, seeping like a stain into our body politic. There has been the indomitable upholding of academic integrity against all intrusions or infractions, no matter how well intentioned, no matter from which quarter.

That is a significant portion of our heritage: the indomitable witness in support of freedom of expression in debate and controversy, no matter how unpopular or unacceptable in some quarters. That witness against ignorance is the great call of our university.

There is another witness in our tradition which invokes nobility of service. We have inherited an expectation that those who have the privilege of coming here to receive an education carry with it a corresponding obligation to society, an obligation not just to do well, but to do good, an obligation to integrate the mind and the heart. Our predecessors were convinced that part of the task the College, and later the University, was to ensure that that debasement did not occur, either to the University or in the lives of those who inhabited it.

For a long time the battle lines seemed to be drawn against forces that seemed to be threatening from outside the College and the University. And those external threats lent a feeling of coherence and commonality to those within the College and the University. Today those threats are not nearly so clear, nor so severe. Our problems today may lie more in our lack of coherence, our loss of faith in the commonality of our work. Ironically, the very means by which our society and our universities have achieved their enormous distinction constitute their Achilles' heel. The rise of specialties, of subdisciplines within the traditional disciplines, has largely removed the possibility of a shared discourse and common values.

Couple the effects of this fragmentation of knowledge with the narrow-minded careerist expectations that pervade our society, and you have a crisis of conscience within the academy. Its sense of purpose that was once so clear, so compelling, so essential to its survival, is missing. So the University — all universities — faces an erosion of meaning.

Surely we are more than an academic holding company, a privileged field of inquiry for independent disciplines and congeries of specialties. Surely there is still the possibility of having a company of scholars, both old and young. Surely, as we look in appreciation upon the spirit that has brought us to this day, we will see our Sesquicentennial as a good time to reaffirm the many steps that we have undertaken recently to counteract the centrifugal tendencies in our academic world.

Every school and division in the University over the past few years has taken steps to foster a challenging reexamination of the patterns of inquiry and of career expectations, the professional standards and assumptions and inducements that have so seductively risen in the past thirty years or so. By virtue of our heritage and our privileged role in society, we at Emory have the right and duty to examine the adequacy and validity of those standards, and those assumptions, and those inducements.

We do not of course have a full understanding of how we should go about doing this. There is no ready blue-print, no plan that we can follow in remodeling our University. But we know that the University has purposes beyond the interest of all of the professionals put together. That it has purposes that drive from the larger company of scholars as they exist here, and as they extend across the generations. It is the challenge of this generation at Emory to go on challenging the new prevailing orthodoxies — many of which today ironically lie within, not outside, the academy — in our disciplines and departments.

Recent grants to Emory from the Henry Luce and the Mellon foundations are funding our initiatives to institute a conversation across the disciplines at Emory about those fundamental questions about human existence that illumine all of our work in whatever fields. What we are asking for is greater intellectual ferment, not less.

We want to also reemphasize the role of the teacher at Emory. This is not a rhetorical flourish prompted by the recent Report of the Carnegie Endowment for Teaching. Most of the faculty sitting in here entered the university initially because we really like to teach. We like to do research, we like to study, we like to write, at least most of us try to write, but we also like to teach. We treasure the moments of seeing people come alive with the thrill of a new idea, the joy of a discovery. And we agree, at least implicitly, with Plato that teaching is essentially a remarkable chemistry between people, not unlike the magic of parenting, in its own proper way ... and with proper qualifications. This relationship between student and teacher is not limited to the undergraduate experience. It is evidenced in the relationship between graduate student and dissertation adviser, resident and physician, clerk and supreme court justice, to name but a few. All of these revolve around that remarkable and very difficult-to-understand attraction. It is precious for an upcoming generation to participate in that chemistry and in that attraction. And when it is denied or overly bureaucratized, the students are frustrated and angry. At Emory we have tried to create the settings where the proper chemistry can occur. We need to work harder now, to create the reward structure, the incentives, that will enable us to foster the richest possible amalgam of marvelous teaching and the deepest and most rigorous scholarship.

As we think back on the beginning of Emory, on the spirit of derring-do that marked those early pioneers, on their remarkable investment in the building of this institution, I would hope we can feel ourselves to be part of the institution that they founded. The great cloud of witnesses over the past 150 years would no doubt be impressed, maybe even awed by what we are doing today, by the facilities and the various centers and programs. I would also hope that upon close inspection they would give us their respect and maybe, upon real knowledge, give us their blessing.

# AN EMORY CHRONOLOGY

1836 The Georgia General Assembly gives the Georgia Methodist Conference a charter to establish a college named for John Emory.

1837 Phi Gamma, the first literary society, is founded; Ignatius Few is elected first president of Emory College; the first faculty members — Alexander Means, George W. Lane, Archelaus Mitchell and George Round, all Methodist preachers — are appointed by the trustees.

1838 Classes begin on September 17 for fifteen students.

1840 Augustus Longstreet becomes second Emory president.

1841 Emory graduates first three students.

1848 George Foster Pierce becomes the third Emory president.

1852 Work begins on a new main building at Oxford, to provide space for a library, science demonstrations, classes and auditorium.

1854 Alexander Means becomes the fourth president of Emory; The Atlanta Medical College is founded.

1855 James R. Thomas becomes the fifth president of Emory.

1857 Fraternities are banned by President Thomas.

1859 All Emory dormitories are closed, cited as "facilities for mischief."

1861 In November Emory closes its doors; During the war the unused buildings were used first as Confederate hospitals and later by Northern occupation troops; 35 Emory men lose their lives in the war.

1866 Emory is re-opened with 20 students and three professors.

1867 Luther Smith becomes sixth president of Emory College.

1871 Osborn L. Smith becomes seventh president of Emory.

1875 Atticus Haygood becomes Emory's eighth president.

1880 George Seney gives $130,000 to Emory, part of which is used to construct Seney Hall; The *Emory Mirror* is first published.

1884 Isaac Hopkins becomes Emory's ninth president.

1888 President Hopkins becomes head of the Georgia School of Technology; Warren Candler becomes tenth president of Emory.

1889 First bachelor of laws degree conferred.

1891 Intercollegiate sports banned at Emory; KA's receive permission to build first fraternity house on campus.

1893 *The Zodiac*, Emory's first yearbook, appears.

1898 Charles Dowman becomes the eleventh president of Emory.

1902 James Dickey becomes Emory's twelfth president; 1902 class is the first to wear caps and gowns at graduation.

1904 Pierce Science Hall completed at Oxford.

1905 Wesley Memorial Hospital's nursing training school established, providing the foundation for Emory University's School of Nursing.

1914 The School of Theology opens; renamed Candler School of Theology in 1915 in honor of the Bishop.

1915 Emory University receives its charter; Asa Candler's Druid Hills Company deeds 75 acres known as the Guess Place to Emory; The Atlanta Medical College becomes Emory's School of Medicine.

1916 The Lamar College of Law is established; the law college and the theology school move into the first two Druid Hills campus buildings.

1917 Eleonore Raoul becomes the first woman admitted to the University; the "Emory Unit," a medical unit, is established in Blois, France.

1919 *The Emory Wheel* is published; Emory College joins the law, theology and pre-clinical programs on the Druid Hills campus; the School of Business Administration and Graduate School are founded.

1920 Harvey W. Cox becomes the first president of Emory University.

1922 Wesley Memorial Hospital, forerunner of Emory University Hospital, moves to a new building on Druid Hills campus.

1924 *The Emory Alumnus* (later *Emory Magazine*) published.

1926 The Asa G. Candler Library dedicated.

1927 SAE's begin construction of first fraternity row house.

1931 Glenn Memorial Church completed and dedicated.

1936 Emory marks its Centennial with ten-day celebration.

1937 Haygood-Hopkins Memorial Gateway built.

1941 Following death of Bishop Candler, first University-sponsored dance occurs; Dooley's Frolics begin, as does World War II in December

1942 Goodrich C. White becomes second Emory University president.

1944 Atlanta-Southern Dental College becomes the Emory School of Dentistry; the Nursing School begins to offer collegiate program.

1946 Post-War enrollment soars to 3,583; 189 new faculty added.

1948 First Ph.D. degree awarded to Thomas P. Johnston in chemistry.

1953 Emory College officially becomes co-educational.

1955 New Administration Building opens, completing the Quadrangle.

1957 Sidney W. Martin becomes third Emory University president.

1958 University purchases Lullwater Estate from Candler family

1963 Sanford Atwood becomes fourth University president.

1966 University renames the medical complex for Robert Woodruff.

1967 Wonderful Wednesdays begin.

1969 Woodruff Library for Advanced Studies is dedicated.

1972 Gilbert Hall becomes Emory's first co-ed dormitory; one millionth volume added to university libraries.

1973 Gambrell Hall, School of Law opens.

1974 The ROTC unit at Emory deactivated.

1975 Dumas Malone becomes first Emory alumnus to win a Pulitzer.

1977 James T. Laney named Emory University's fifth president; Goodrich White Hall opens; David Potter wins Pulitzer in History.

1979 Emory receives $105 million from the Emily and Ernest Woodruff Fund, the largest single educational gift in American history; President Jimmy Carter delivers address at groundbreaking of Cannon Chapel; the renovated Houston Mill House opens to serve as center for University social functions.

1982 Former President Carter joins Emory faculty; Alumnus C. Vann Woodward wins Pulitzer Prize in History; University calendar changed to a semester system, eliminating Wonderful Wednesdays.

1983 Woodruff Physical Education Center opens; Turman Residential Center opens; alumnus Claude Sitton wins Pulitzer for Commentary.

1984 Alumnus Louis Harlan wins Pulitzer Prize in Biography; at the end of the five-year Campaign for Emory, $220 million has been raised, $60 million more than original goal.

1985 Renovation of the Old Law Building completed and named for benefactor Michael C. Carlos; Emory Transplant Center performs first heart transplant; philanthropist Robert W. Woodruff dies.

1986 Emory celebrates its Sesquicentennial; varsity basketball begins; O. Wayne Rollins pledges $10 million to start new life sciences research center; Carter Presidential Center dedicated, with President Reagan in attendance; first phase of the R. Howard Dobbs University Center completed; George and Irene Woodruff Residential Center breaks ground; Boisfeuillet Jones Center is dedicated.

1987 Two-millionth volume added to library holdings; the University's 150th Anniversary concludes with graduation of Class of 1987.

*Mantle, Dobbs Hall*

*What was needed to counter the centrifugal forces at work in our culture was some intentional pressure, some plan for how life within the university could be brought into a new coherence. And that coherence was what I described as a "community of scholars." Now this concept suggests more than simply a warm place where students and teachers can feel comfortable with each other. It does not prescribe some cloying principle of organizational control. It suggests a restless, vital, creative collection of talents and energies enriching each other and releasing far more powerful intellectual and moral forces than could ever emerge out of isolated faculties.*

Dr. James T. Laney, President, Emory University, 1985

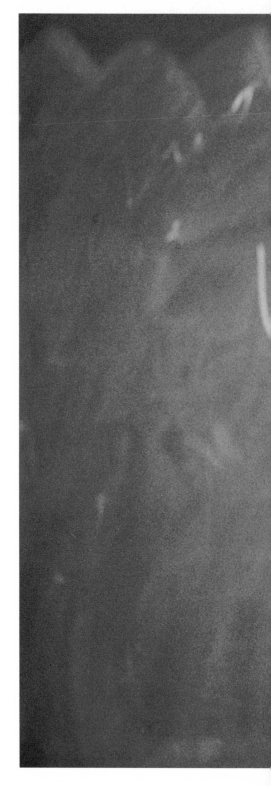

*Overleaf: The Pitts Theology Library*

25

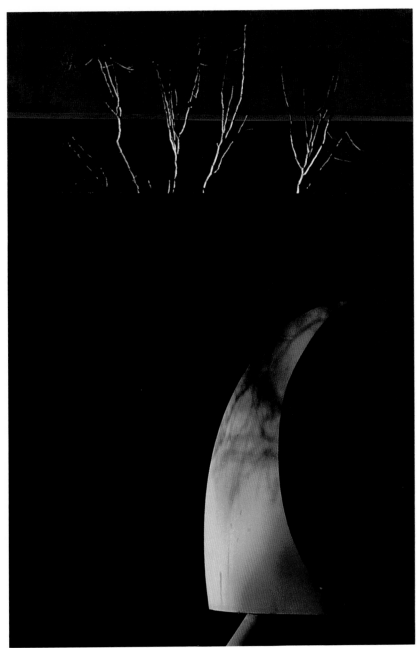

*"The Wave," by Jim Clover, Goodrich C. White Hall*

*Overleaf: The Law School, Gambrell Hall*

*Howard Dobbs University Center*

*Each year that goes by I recognize more what a fine education Emory University provides. Being a graduate of Emory University Law School is indeed something to be proud of. I believe the School of Law at Emory University provided me with an excellent foundation for practicing law in Perry, Georgia and for serving in the United States Senate.*

Senator Sam Nunn, '61C, '62L

*Distinguished Alumni Gallery, Law School*

*The School of Law, Gambrell Hall*

*I would vote for the campus of Emory University
as the most beautiful in America...Visiting Emory
was like walking into the Garden of Eden.*

Alistair Cooke, on BBC broadcast,"Letter
from America," November 1977

The Quadrangle

*Lullwater Estate*

*Our most pressing job was to place the entire academic program upon such a sound basis that an Emory diploma would carry prestige wherever sound scholarship is recognized and valued.*

Harvey W. Cox, Alumni Report, 1942

*Asa Griggs Candler Library*

*Overleaf: Angioplasty procedure, Emory University Hospital*

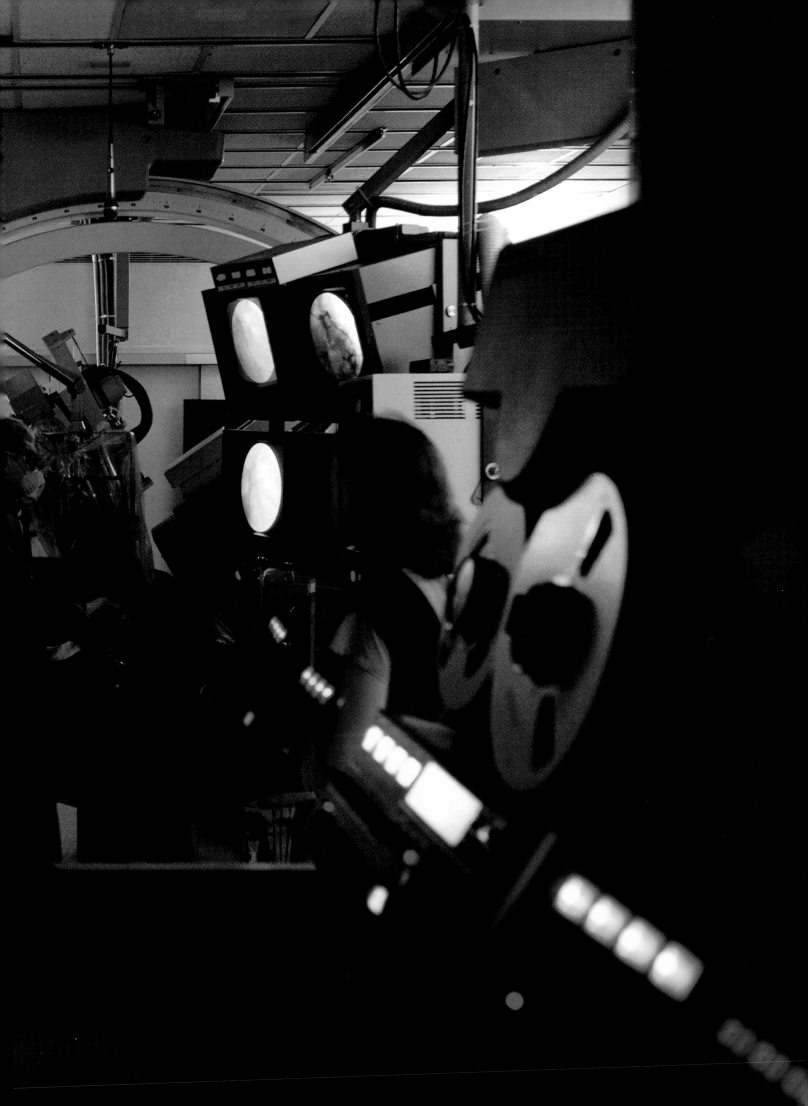

Education is fundamental to the well-being of society. Emory University and Emory College at Oxford have demonstrated leadership in educational service for nearly a century and a half. Trustees of the Emily and Ernest Woodruff Fund...have observed development of the University for 40 years and provided substantial support for it from time to time.

Gratified by Emory's progress, its demonstrated capacity to manage its affairs, and its continued commitment to educational excellence in the service of society, trustees of the Emily and Ernest Woodruff Fund have determined that resources committed to their care for public benefit can be of greatest potential for service in the South, their area of special interest, if concentrated now in Emory University.

Robert W. Woodruff, 1979

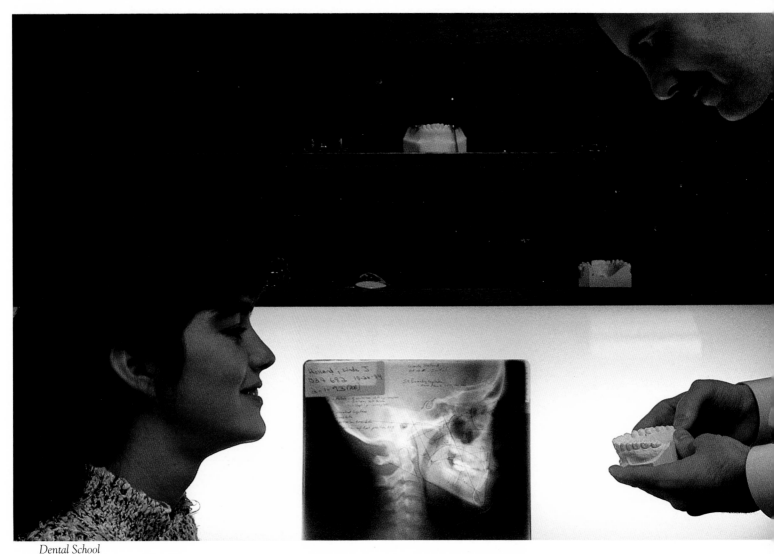

Dental School

*Robert W. Woodruff*

*The Carter Center*

*Education, properly, embraces the whole wide scope of the character, condition, and interests of man, physical, mental, moral and religious, for time and eternity.*

Robert Emory, in *The Life of Bishop Emory*

*Overleaf: The Lullwater Estate*

*President's Home / Lullwater House*

*Their half-timbered and castellated manors certainly look at home on these tree-surrounded, druidical sites. Both look for all the world like stately homes of Tudor England.*

Van Jones Martin, William Mitchell, Jr., in *Landmark Homes of Georgia*

*Lullwater House, interior*

*This is my party.*

Dooley, 1941

An education at Emory involves several distinct elements — intense academic work, strong fraternities, the proximity of Atlanta … Emory, once clearly a regional institution, is now a fine, national university. It is also a place of unrivaled institutional dynamism.

Edward B. Fiske, in *The Selective Guide to Colleges*

*Party, Fraternity Row*

George W. Woodruff Physical Education Center

Oxford College, Few Monument

*Emory Village, Haygood-Hopkins Gate*

R. Howard Dobbs University Center, interior

The Quadrangle

*The use of block-form buildings with wide eaves and arched windows in combination with pink and gray Georgia marble slabs in a random quilt-like pattern suggests the Italian villas and buildings of Renaissance Tuscany.*

From *Dooley's Book* (as communicated to G.P. Cuttino)

*Dome, Little Chapel*

*Woodruff Memorial Research Building detail*

*Dome, Dobbs Center*

*Overleaf: Michael C. Carlos Hall*

*Hornbostel's proportions are wonderful and so is his sensitivity to context and site — the way the building relates to its site. There's always a wonderful hierarchy of passage or movement in his buildings.*

Michael Graves, in *Emory* Magazine, March 1985

Michael C. Carlos Hall, interiors

*Day Chapel, Oxford College*

*The traditional Christmas Concert*

*The Old Church, Oxford, Georgia*

*Little Chapel, Glenn Memorial Church*

*Business School, Rich Memorial Building*

*Environmental Nuclear Physics Lab*

*Laser research, Chemistry Building*

Most of the faculty sitting in here entered the university initially because we really like to teach. We like to do research, we like to study, we like to write, at least most of us try to write, but we also like to teach. We treasure the moments of seeing people come alive with the thrill of a new idea, the joy of discovery.

Dr. James T. Laney, Sesquicentennial address

*The Pitts Theology Library*

*DNA research*

## THE COCA-COLA SCHOOL

*We're not allowed a football team*
*That will break through Georgia's line;*
*With all the baseball bull we fling*
*We'll never beat Tech's nine;*
*But our poker teams are winners,*
*Defeat we never fear.*
*So buy your lot and hike the pot;*
*We need your money here.*
*CHORUS:*
*Emory, Emory, thy future we foretell.*
*We were raised on Coca-Cola*
*So no wonder we raise hell.*
*When e'er we meet Tech's engineers,*
*We drink them off their stool.*
*So fill your cup, here's to the luck*
*Of the Coca-Cola School.*

From *The Emory Campus*, 1923

*There can be no possible doubt that the Southeast needs and deserves a university of the highest quality; nor can there be doubt that the entire country would benefit from its existence…In the whole tier of states…no other institution is in a position comparable with that of Emory to become such a university.*

Dumas Malone, '10C, 1945

# A LOOK BACK AT EMORY

*A selection of photographs from the Emory Archives and Special Collections*

The Emory football team gathers for a photograph by Few Hall at the turn of the century. [ *Emory Archives, Special Collections Department, Woodruff Library, Emory University* ]

Ignatius Few represented the Georgia Methodist Conference in its successful attempt to obtain a charter from the Georgia General Assembly for the establishment of a college. With charter granted, and school named (for Bishop John Emory), Few was elected the school's first president in 1837. He served as president until 1839. [ *Emory Archives, Special Collections Department, Woodruff Library, Emory University*].

Few Literary Society Hall on the Oxford campus, site of celebrated speech training for generations of Phi Gammas and other debaters. [ *Emory Archives, Special Collections Department, Woodruff Library, Emory University* ]

The Old Chapel at Oxford, circa 1875. [ *Emory Archives, Special Collections Department, Woodruff Library, Emory University* ]

The Emory University School of Medicine's predecessors included the Atlanta Medical College, founded in 1854, and shown here a few years later. [ *Emory Archives, Special Collections Department, Woodruff Library, Emory University* ].

In 1905 Wesley Memorial Hospital opened in Atlanta, and with it was established a training school for nurses which became a forerunner of Emory's School of Nursing. [ *Emory Archives, Special Collections Department, Woodruff Library, Emory University* ]

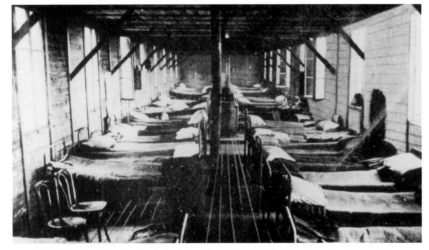

In 1917, Emory medical school faculty and alumni gathered to form the Emory Unit, Base Hospital 43 in Blois, France. [ *Emory Archives, Special Collections Department, Woodruff Library, Emory University* ]

Emory policy in 1919 dictated that freshmen and sophomores be required to participate in the new ROTC unit. [ *Emory Archives, Special Collections Department, Woodruff Library, Emory University]*

This is a 1917 view of the interior of the Law School Library, which was later renovated to become Carlos Hall. [ *Emory Archives, Special Collections Department, Woodruff Library, Emory University* ]

In 1917, Eleonore Raoul became the first woman admitted to Emory University, enrolling in the College of Law. [ *Raoul Family Papers, Special Collections Department, Woodruff Library, Emory University* ].

1923 saw the initiation of a pushball contest between the freshmen and sophomores. [ *Emory Archives, Special Collections Department, Woodruff Library, Emory University* ]

1922 Wesley Memorial Hospital moved to a new building on the Druid Hills campus. In 1925 it was officially transferred to Emory, and within a few ars was known as Emory University Hospital. [ *Emory Archives, Special Collections Department, Woodruff Library, Emory University* ]

Candler Hall, the library at Oxford, circa 1935. [ *Emory Archives, Special Collections Department, Woodruff Library, Emory University* ].

Emory College alumnus and trustee Linton B. Robeson gave the University the Haygood-Hopkins Memorial Gateway in 1937. [ *Emory Archives, Special Collections Department, Woodruff Library, Emory University* ]

This 100,000 gallon water tower, an Emory landmark, was erected in 1933. [ *Emory Archives, Special Collections Department, Woodruff Library, Emory University* ]

Seney Hall at Oxford, circa 1935. The building was funded by George Seney of New York, a descendant of Emory's founder, Ignatius Few. [ *Emory Archives, Special Collections Department, Woodruff Library, Emory University* ]

The Candler Library interior in the 30s. [ *Emory Archives, Special Collections Department, Woodruff Library, Emory University* ]

Glenn Memorial Church was completed in 1931. It was dedicated as a memorial to Wilbur Fisk Glenn, an Emory alumnus and prominent Methodist minister. [ *Emory Archives, Special Collections Department, Woodruff Library, Emory University* ]

Emory was recognized for its contributions to the World War II effort by having this cargo ship christened the *M.S. Emory* in 1945.
[ *Emory Archives, Special Collections Department, Woodruff Library, Emory University* ]

Harris Hall, shown here just after construction in 1930. [ *Emory Archives, Special Collections Department, Woodruff Library, Emory University* ]

In 1953, Emory officially became a coeducational school. In past years women had been admitted in limited circumstances, but in this year a policy was established allowing female enrollment and resident status. [ *Emory Archives, Special Collections Department, Woodruff Library, Emory University* ].

Many Emory alumni will remember signing in and out of Harris Hall. This photo is from the 1950s. [ *Emory Archives, Special Collections Department, Woodruff Library, Emory University* ]

In 1975, alumnus and historian Dumas Malone became Emory's first Pulitzer Prize winner, for the first five volumes of his Thomas Jefferson biography, *Jefferson and His Time*. [ *Photograph by John Foraste, Emory Archives, Special Collections Department, Woodruff Library, Emory University* ]

Alumnus Claude Sitton, editor of the *Raleigh News and Observer*, won a Pulitzer Prize for journalistic commentary in 1983. [ *Emory Archives, Special Collections Department, Woodruff Library, Emory University* ]

In 1984, alumnus Louis Harlan won the Pulitzer Prize in biography for his work, *Booker T. Washington: The Wizard of Tuskegee, 1901-1915.* [ *Emory Archives, Special Collections Department, Woodruff Library, Emory University* ]

The Pulitzer Prize in history for 1982 went to Emory alumnus C. Vann Woodward for his work, *Mary Chestnut's Civil War.*
[ *Photograph by Billy Howard, Emory Archives, Special Collections Department, Woodruff Library, Emory University* ]

George Cuttino, Candler Professor of Medieval History, Emeritus, and Jerry Finegan, Emory's first official bagpiper.

Students toast the end of "Wonderful Wednesdays" in 1982. [ *Photograph by Billy Howard* ]

Business leader, philanthropist and Emory benefactor Robert W. Woodruff is shown in 1981 with Emory President James T. Laney and Gina Greco, one of the first eleven Woodruff Scholars in Emory College. [*Photograph by Billy Howard*]